FIRST BO OF MATHS

Annabel Thomas and Nigel Langdon
Designed and illustrated by Graham Round

Contents
Pages 2-32: Multiplying and Dividing

- 2 First times
- 4 Hops and jumps
- 6 Tables time
- 8 Bigtum's patterns
- 10 Sharing
- 12 Left overs
- 14 Paper sums
- 16 Decimals
- 18 Calculator fun
- 20 Special numbers
- 22 Big sums
- 24 Percentages
- 26 Tables tips
- 28 Treasure hunt
- 30 Answers
- 32 Answers
  Toby's table square

Pages 33-63: Weighing and Measuring
Page 64: Index

Edited by Helen Davies
Subject consultants: Geoff Sheath and Ruth Tolhurst

First times

Multiplication is a quick way of adding a number over and over again. Dodo and Dogosaurus show you how this works.

Dodo has 3 bunches of balloons. There are 5 in each bunch so she has 3 sets of 5. You can write this as 5 × 3

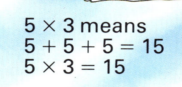

5 × 3 means
5 + 5 + 5 = 15
5 × 3 = 15

(5 multiplied by 3). The × is the multiplication sign.* Three sets of 5 make 15, so 5 × 3 = 15.

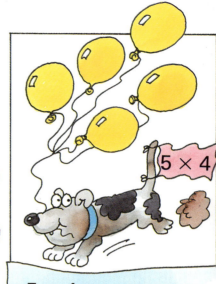

5 × 4 means
5 + 5 + 5 + 5 = 20
5 × 4 = 20

If Dogosaurus adds another bunch there are 4 sets of 5, or 5 balloons multiplied by 4. This is written as 5 × 4.

Try these

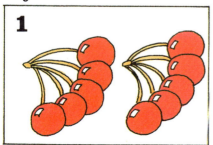

1 How many sets of 5 chewy cherries are there above? Can you write a multiplication sum for them?

2 Monster warblers

Count how many monster warblers there are in each nest. Then try writing a multiplication sum for them.

3 See if you can write a multiplication sum for the flowers Dodo has given to her mum.

*The × is often called the "times" sign, too, because 5 multiplied by 3 is 5, 3 times.

Bigtum's shopping expedition

SHOPPING LIST

2 trays of monstermallows. How many is that?

3 boxes of orangofruits. How many orangofruits altogether?

5 packets of snappercrackers. How many altogether?

2 bags of monsterchox. How many monsterchox is that?

On the right is Bigtum's shopping list. Can you work out how many of each item he buys, by writing a multiplication sum for each item on the list?

Using multiplication

Multiplication can speed up lots of calculations. For instance, Slimy Sid's Aunty Mabel gives each of her 8 children 4 munchies a week. (Munchies are monster money.) What is a quick way to find how many munchies she needs altogether?

Hops and jumps

Another way to do multiplication is by using a number line. Snout and Toadie show you how in this picture.

$4 \times 3 = 12$

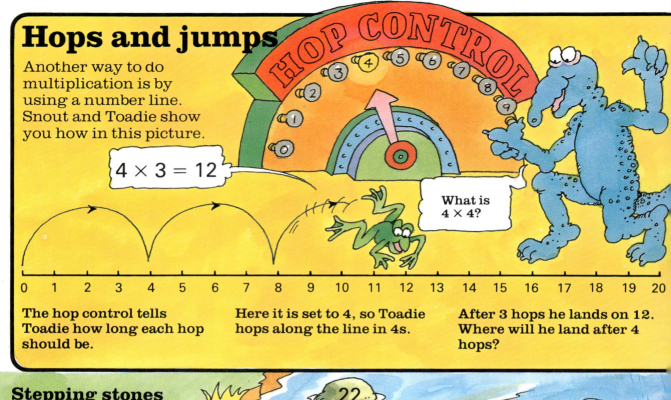

The hop control tells Toadie how long each hop should be.

Here it is set to 4, so Toadie hops along the line in 4s.

After 3 hops he lands on 12. Where will he land after 4 hops?

Stepping stones

Grumble and Snout are playing stepping stones across the river. Stones 18 and 20 have sunk into the river bed. Imagine they are going to start on 0 and hop in equal-size hops along the line of the stones. What length of hop will they need to make to avoid the two missing stones?

Snout has made Toadie some number lines to hop along. Some of them have halves on, too. Can you do the same and then use them to solve how far Toadie leaps?

Leap frog

1 The hop control is set to 2. Which number will Toadie land on after 3 hops? Complete the multiplication:

$2 \times 3 =$

2 Try hopping in 2s and see if you can do these multiplications.

$2 \times 4 = \qquad 2 \times 5 = \qquad 2 \times 6 =$

3 Change the hop size to $3\frac{1}{2}$ and try these sums.

$3\frac{1}{2} \times 2 = \qquad 3\frac{1}{2} \times 3 =$

4 See if you can fill in the missing numbers in these rows. Use a number line to help you.

0, 3, 6, ★, 12, 15, ★
0, 7, ★
0, ★, 8, 12, ★, ★ ← Missing numbers

Which way round?

$3 \times 4 = 12$

$4 \times 3 = 12$

$3 \times 4 = 4 \times 3$

Try 2×6 and 6×2.

These smellyjellies could be counted by saying there are 4 different coloured sets with 3 in each. So, $3 \times 4 = 12$.

Or you could say there are 3 different shaped sets with 4 smellyjellies in each. So, $4 \times 3 = 12$.

The order in which you multiply two numbers does not matter because you always get the same answer.

Tables time

Tables are lists showing what you get when you multiply one number by 0 to 10. Here Snout is showing Toadie the 3s table. On pages 26-27 you can meet Toby T. Table, the monster tables champion, and all the tables from 0 to 10.

3s table

3 × 0 = 0
3 × 1 = 3
3 × 2 = 6
3 × 3 = 9
3 × 4 = 12
3 × 5 = 15
3 × 6 = 18
3 × 7 = 21
3 × 8 = 24
3 × 9 = 27
3 × 10 = 30

Look Toadie! These are the numbers you land on when you jump along a number line in 3s. They are called the multiples of 3.

3 × 0 is 0
3 × 1 is 3
3 × 2 is 6
3 × 3 is 9

Grumble is learning his tables off by heart so he can do multiplication quickly. There are hints and a fun computer program to help *you* learn them on pages 26-29.

Bigtum's monster cake

Don't forget, you can use the tables on pages 26-27 to help you.

5 squirts of greasy goo
8 blobs of pink puffs
6 blobs of crazy crunch
2 dinosaur eggs
7 blobs of sherbert fizz
10 chocolate bubbles
4 squirts of cream

Monsters measure weight in blobs, and volume in squirts.

Bigtum wants to make a giant monster cake 4 times as big as the one in this recipe. How much of each ingredient will he need?

The monsters' magic tables spiral

All the monsters have one of these. Follow the instructions and you can, too.

This spiral shows the 4s table.

1 The lines should go across the strip.

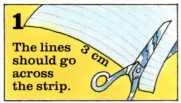

Cut a strip of lined paper about 3cm by 30cm.

2

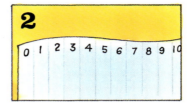

Write numbers between the lines along one edge, starting at 0.

3 The numbers should be on the outside of the roll.

Turn the strip over and roll it up, starting at the opposite end from 0.

4

Loosen or tighten the roll so 0 lines up with, say, 4.

5 Use a pencil to push the spiral up.

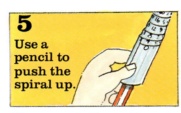

Then push the roll up to make a spiral showing the 4s table, as above.

6

For a new table, adjust the roll until a new number lines up with 0.

How heavy is Ugly Mug?

Use the tables on pages 26-27 to help you work out these puzzles.

Ugly Mug is 9 times heavier than he was as a baby. As a baby he weighed 5 kiloblobs.* How many kiloblobs does he weigh now?

Party puzzle

Headcase brews sparkling party juice. The monsters drink 7 bottles at each party. How many bottles must she make for 6 parties?

*1 kiloblob is 1000 blobs.

Bigtum's patterns

Bigtum has discovered he can make circle patterns using multiplication tables. See how he does it below. You need paper and coloured pencils and something circular (a cup or a jar) to draw round.

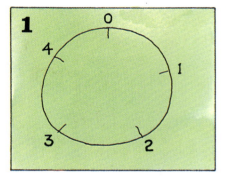

1 Draw a circle and mark five points round the edge like this. Number them 0 to 4 with 0 at the top.

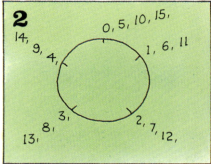

2 Carry on numbering the points round the circle to 15. Put your pencil on 0 and jump across the circle in 3s.

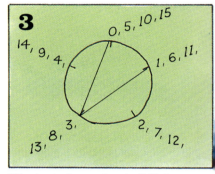

3 Bigtum has started this circle. Can you finish it for him to see what pattern jumping in 3s makes?

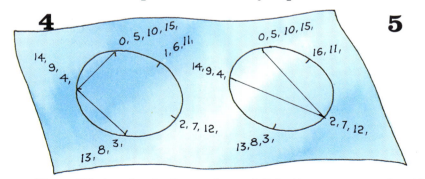

4 Draw Bigtum's circle again and this time jump across it in 4s, or 2s or 6s. What patterns do you get? You may need to add more numbers round the circle to complete the patterns.

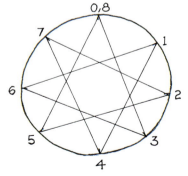

5 See if you can make a more complicated pattern than Bigtum's. For instance, try drawing a circle with 8 points. Two tables could have been used to make this pattern. Which are they?

Square patterns

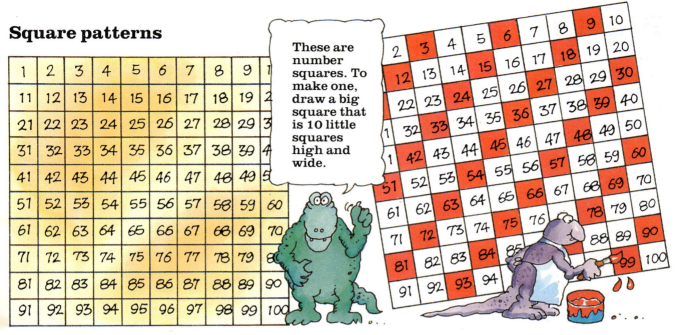

These are number squares. To make one, draw a big square that is 10 little squares high and wide.

If you put all the numbers from 1 to 100 into the squares like this, you can colour in the multiples of different numbers and get some interesting patterns.

Crosseyes got this pattern by colouring the multiples of 3. You could try other multiples, such as 4, 5 or 7. Experiment to see which multiples make the best pattern.

Tens trick

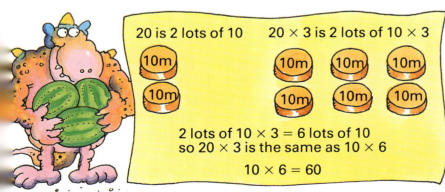

20 is 2 lots of 10

20 × 3 is 2 lots of 10 × 3

2 lots of 10 × 3 = 6 lots of 10
so 20 × 3 is the same as 10 × 6

10 × 6 = 60

Here is a trick for multiplying big numbers, such as 20. Lazylump is buying 3 slimelons at 20 munchies each. To find out how much money he needs, think of 20 as 2 lots of 10 and use your tables to find the answer.

Tens puzzle

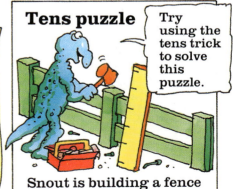

Try using the tens trick to solve this puzzle.

Snout is building a fence using planks 40 trotters long. (Monsters measure in trotters.) She needs 2 planks. How long will the fence be?

Sharing

Three of the monsters are playing Snappy Families. The game starts by them sharing out 6 cards, so they each get 2. Sharing equally is called dividing. Division sums are written with this sign ÷. It means "divided by".

$6 ÷ 3 = 2$

$15 ÷ 3$

$15 ÷ 3 = 5$

Grumble is working out $15 ÷ 3$. He arranges 15 buttons in 3 equal sets and counts how many there are in each set. Try using buttons or coins, like this, to solve the puzzles below.

1

Chopitup has 8 juicy bones to share equally between his 2 dogs, Yapper and Snapper. How many bones does each dog get?

2

Bigtum has been on holiday. He has brought back 9 sticks of rock to give to his 3 friends. How many sticks does each one get?

3

There are 20 jellybean seeds in Bristlebag's packet and she has 5 pots to plant them in. How many seeds will there be in each pot?

Headcase and the chocobars

Headcase has 12 munchies to spend on chocobars. One bar costs 4 munchies. How many bars can she buy with her money?

$12 \div 4 = 3$

Headcase worked out the answer by finding out how many groups of 4 there are in 12. She drew 12 dots to represent the munchies. Then she put rings round groups of 4. How many groups of 4 are there?

Get a pencil and paper and try working out these divisions by drawing rings round groups of dots, like Headcase did.

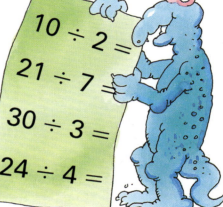

$10 \div 2 =$
$21 \div 7 =$
$30 \div 3 =$
$24 \div 4 =$

Hopping backwards

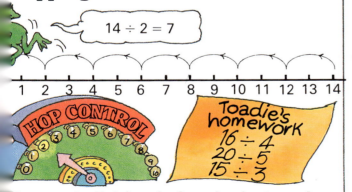

$14 \div 2 = 7$

Toadie's homework
$16 \div 4$
$20 \div 5$
$15 \div 3$

You can do divisions by hopping backwards on a number line. Here Toadie is finding out the answer to $14 \div 2$. Can you see how many hops of 2 it takes him to get from 14 back to 0? Try using a number line to solve the rest of Toadie's homework.

Multiplication and division

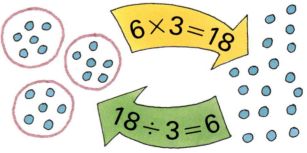

$6 \times 3 = 18$

$18 \div 3 = 6$

Division is the opposite of multiplication. Three groups of 6 make 18 altogether and if you divide 18 into three groups you have 6 in each group. $18 \div 3 = 6$ because $6 \times 3 = 18$.

Left overs

Sometimes a number cannot be divided exactly. Here, the monsters show you what to do when this happens.

$36 \div 5 =$
$84 \div 9 =$
$42 \div 7 =$
$55 \div 6 =$
$28 \div 3 =$

$13 \div 2 = 6$ remainder 1

Ugly Mug tries to share out 13 monsterbles with Snout. They each get 6 monsterbles, but there is 1 left over. Left overs are called remainders.

Some of the sums on the wall above leave remainders. Try them and see.

Ugly Mug's pretty patterns

The lines go downwards

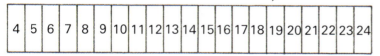

To make Ugly Mug's patterns, cut a strip of lined paper like this. Number the lines starting with 4. (You could start with any number between 0 and 10.)

Divide each number by 4. Colour numbers with a remainder of 1, red, numbers with a remainder of 2, blue, numbers with a remainder of 3, another colour and so on. After each multiple of 4, the pattern repeats itself. Try beginning the line with other numbers to see the different patterns you get.

Brain teaser

A pack of 36 cards is dealt out between a group of monsters and there are none left over. Then another friend joins in. This time there is one card left over when the pack is dealt. How many monsters are now playing cards?

Bits and pieces

Sometimes you can divide remainders into parts, called fractions.

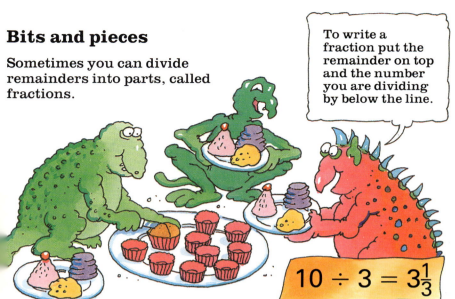

To write a fraction put the remainder on top and the number you are dividing by below the line.

$10 \div 3 = 3\frac{1}{3}$

Dodo shares out 10 cakes with Bigtum and Slimy Sid. They each get 3, but there is one left. So she cuts it into three equal parts.

Each part is called a third, written $\frac{1}{3}$. This means 1 divided by 3. So they each get $3\frac{1}{3}$ cakes.

One more cake

If Dodo had had to share 11 cakes, they would each have had $3\frac{2}{3}$ cakes. How could the left over cakes have been cut?

Monsterous problems

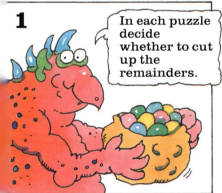

In each puzzle decide whether to cut up the remainders.

1 This is Bigtum's weekly supply of gobstoppers. There are 39 in the bag. How many does he have for each day of the week?

2 Slimy Sid is playing cowboys and indians. He cuts a 13 trotter rope into 2 equal pieces to tie up his friends. How long is each piece?

3 Snout takes 49 seconds to trot round the race track five times. If she always trots at the same pace, how long does it take her to go round once?

Paper sums

Sometimes you need to multiply and divide numbers on paper, like Snout and Bigtum are doing, because they are too large to do in your head. But beware! The monsters are working out monster time sums. See the monster time chart on the right.

Multiplying

1 MONSTER TIME
1 week = 3 days
1 month = 27 days
1 year = 6 months

Hundreds column → H
Tens column → T
Units column → U

```
  H T U
    2 7
  ×   6
  ─────
```

+ (7 × 6)
  (20 × 6)

The sum on the left is equal to the sum on the right.

Toadie wants to know how many days in a monster year and so must multiply 27 by 6. He thinks of 27 as 20 + 7 and then multiplies both parts by 6. He writes down the sum and then gets stuck, so Brainy monster shows him how to do it on the right.

Dividing

1
3 × 1 = 3
3 × 10 = 30
3 × 2 = 6
3 × 20 = 60
3 × 3 = 9
3 × 30 = 90

Dividing is like doing repeated subtraction. Here Toadie is working out how many monster weeks in 67 monster days. So he sets out the sum 67 ÷ 3, as shown above. To work out

The answer goes here.

3) 67

By checking 3 × 20 and 3 × 30 you can see that the answer lies between 20 and 30.

the answer, he needs to take away as many lots of 3 as possible, using the 3s table to help him. Toadie explains how you can do this too, on the right.

2
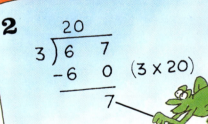

```
     20
  ┌─────
3 ) 6 7
   -6 0    (3 × 20)
   ─────
     7
```

7 are left to be divided.

The 3s table shows that 20 lots of 3 can be subtracted from 67. You put the 20 above the line and then take away 60 from 67.

2 Take care to put the numbers in the right columns.

```
  H T U
    2 7
  ×   6
  ─────
      2
    4
```

Brainy says, first multiply the units. 7 × 6 is 42 which is 4 tens and 2 units. Put the 2 in the units column and carry the 4 tens to the tens column so that you can use them later.

3

```
  H T U
    2 7
  ×   6
  ─────
  1 6 2
    4
```

There are 162 days in a monster year.

Now multiply the tens. 2 tens × 6 is 12 tens. Add the 4 tens waiting to the 12 tens. Now you have 16 tens. That is 160. Put the 6 tens in the tens column and the 1 hundred in the hundreds column.

Bigger numbers

Thousands column →

```
  Th H T U
     3 2 7
  ×      6
  ────────
   1 9 6 2
     1 4
```

You can multiply even bigger numbers in the same way. In this sum you think of 327 as being made up of 300 + 20 + 7. All three parts are multiplied by 6 and added together.

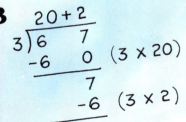

```
       20 + 2
    ┌─────────
  3 │ 6  7
    - 6  0     (3 × 20)
    ─────
         7
       - 6     (3 × 2)
       ───
         1
```

The answer is 22 (20 + 2) remainder 1.

Two lots of 3 can be subtracted from 7. So add the 2 to the 20 above the line and take away 6 from 7. This leaves a remainder of 1.

Bigger divisions

```
         30 + 4 = 34
      ┌─────────────
   4  │ 1 3 8
      - 1 2 0        (4 × 30)
      ───────
          1 8
        - 1 6        (4 × 4)
        ─────
            2
```

The answer is 34 remainder 2.

You work out bigger divisions in exactly the same way. In this sum 34 lots of 4 can be subtracted from 138, by first taking away 30 lots of 4 and then 4 lots of 4.

Headcase's holiday

Don't forget to work in monster time.

Headcase has to wait 3 monster months before she goes on holiday. How many monster weeks is that? Slimy Sid's holiday is not for another 25 monster weeks and 2 monster days. How many days is that?

Decimals

The monsters are multiplying and dividing decimal fractions, or decimals for short. Decimal fractions are numbers smaller than one. They are made up of tenths, hundredths and so on and are joined on to whole numbers with a dot called a decimal point.

The 6 stands for 6 tenths and the 5 stands for 5 hundredths.

Over the page you can find out how to multiply and divide decimals on a calculator.

Often time has to be measured very accurately. In the Monster Olympics, for example, all the races are timed to a hundredth of a second.

Changing remainders into decimals

$4 \times 7 = 28$
So $4 \times 0.7 = 2.8$

```
           7 · 7 5    ← Tenths
         _____     ← Hundredths
      4 ) 3 1
        - 2 8         (4 × 7)
        _____
          3 · 0
        - 2 · 8       (4 × 0.7)
        _____
          0 · 2 0
        - 0 · 2 0     (4 × 0·05)
        _____
          0 · 0 0
```

$4 \times 5 = 20$
So $4 \times 0.5 = 2$
So $4 \times 0.05 = 0.2$

Aunty Mabel's knitting

Try changing the remainder into a decimal fraction.

Slimy Sid's Aunty Mabel has knitted him a stripey scarf. It is 44 trotters long and has 5 equal stripes. How long is each stripe?

Here, Toadie shows how you can change a remainder into a decimal fraction. By adding columns for tenths and hundredths you can turn the remainders into tenths and hundredths. Then you can carry on dividing to make a decimal fraction.

Multiplying decimals

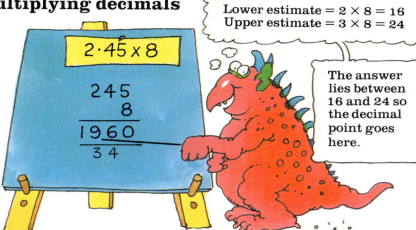

2·45 x 8
245
8
1960
34
Lower estimate = 2 × 8 = 16
Upper estimate = 3 × 8 = 24
The answer lies between 16 and 24 so the decimal point goes here.

You multiply decimal fractions as if they were whole numbers, without the decimal point. To find out where the decimal point goes in the answer, you need to work out an upper and lower estimate, as Bigtum is doing.

Grumble's bubble gum

BUBBLE GUM IS COOL

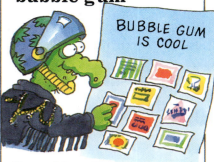

Grumble collects bubble gum wrappers. He has 9 altogether. Each bubble gum costs him 1.5 munchies. Can you work out how much he has spent on his collection?

Toadie's dividing tip

$$28 \div 0{\cdot}4$$

To divide by a decimal, first make it into a whole number, like this.

$$0{\cdot}4 \times 10 = 4$$

Next multiply the number being divided by the same amount.

$$28 \times 10 = 280$$

Then do a division sum with the whole numbers.

$$\begin{array}{r} 70 \\ 4\overline{)280} \\ -280 \\ \hline 000 \end{array} \quad (4 \times 70)$$

Ugly Mug's matching game

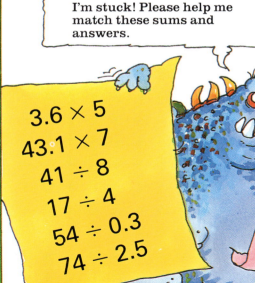

I'm stuck! Please help me match these sums and answers.
3.6 × 5
43.1 × 7
41 ÷ 8
17 ÷ 4
54 ÷ 0.3
74 ÷ 2.5
301.7
180
4.25
29.6
18
5.125

Calculator fun

Aunty Mabel has given Snout a calculator for her birthday. The monsters have discovered how to multiply and divide on it already. See how below.

It is best to check the answer in your head in case you make a mistake. Bigtum shows you how, below.

All you have to do is press the keys for the first number. Then press the multiplication or division sign, and then the keys for the second number. Finally, press the equals key and hey presto, the answer appears in the display panel! Before doing a new sum, press the "clear" key, usually marked C. This wipes the last sum from the calculator.

Checking the answer

It is easy to press the wrong key on a calculator, especially if your fingers are as big as Ugly Mug's. So, before doing a sum, monsters always estimate the size of the answer in their heads. To do this they round off the numbers to the nearest ten, hundred, or thousand. Then they multiply or divide them.

Try these

The monsters have worked out some sums for you to try. Estimate the answers to them first. If an estimate is very different from the calculator answer, check both calculations.

67 ÷ 2
143 ÷ 5
3726 ÷ 9
276 × 7
1250 × 4
53 × 9

On a calculator, remainders are given as decimals. Sometimes the remainder will not divide exactly and the calculator carries on dividing until the answer fills the display.

Games and guesses

1

Snout is working out the biggest and smallest number that can be made using the multiplication sign and these numbers. Can you?

2

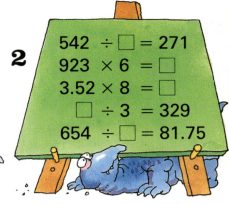

$542 \div \square = 271$
$923 \times 6 = \square$
$3.52 \times 8 = \square$
$\square \div 3 = 329$
$654 \div \square = 81.75$

Snout's friend, Snooty, thinks you won't be able to work out the missing numbers in his sums. Can you?

3

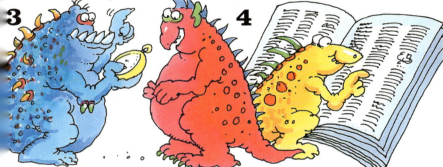

Ugly Mug and Bigtum are finding out how many times they breathe in a day. You can do the same if you follow the hints below.

Hints

Count the number of times you breathe in a minute. Multiply this by the number of minutes in an hour and then multiply by the number of hours in a day.

4

Creep is using a dictionary to find out how many monster words there are. Below there are hints on how to count English words.

Hints

Count the number of words on one page of an English dictionary and multiply by the number of pages in the book.

Snout's number trick

Here is a trick that will amaze and astound your friends. Ask a friend to think of a number, but not tell you what it is. Then ask them to do the following calculations on a calculator.*

Add 3 to the number	$+\ 3$
Multiply by 2	$\times\ 2$
Add 12	$+\ 12$
Multiply by 3	$\times\ 3$
Take away 18	$-\ 18$
Divide by 6	$\div\ 6$
Press equals key	$=$

Do not press clear key

Now take the calculator from your friend and do the following calculations.

Take away 6	
Press equals key	

Your answer will be the number your friend first thought of.

*If you use a scientific calculator, press the equals key after each part of the calculation.

Special numbers

There are some special kinds of numbers you may not have heard of before, such as factors, primes and squares. The monster gang have some tips on how to spot them and suggestions for ways to use them.

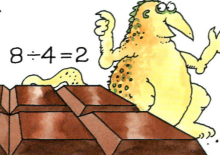

2 and 4 are factors of 8 and 8 is a multiple of 2 and 4.

$8 \div 2 = 4$

$8 \div 4 = 2$

The factors of a number are all the numbers that divide into it without leaving a remainder. For instance, 2 and 4 are factors of 8 because they divide into 8 exactly. You can see this is true from looking at Headcase's monsterchoc. Can you think of two more factors of 8?

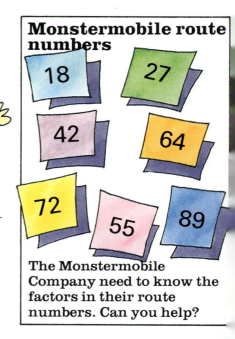

Monstermobile route numbers

18   27   42   64   72   55   89

The Monstermobile Company need to know the factors in their route numbers. Can you help?

True or false?

7 is a factor of 21

4 is a factor of 37

9 is a factor of 81

Ugly Mug   Snout   Headcase

Which of these monsters are telling the truth?

Monstermobile bus

Monstermobiles have 24 seats. The seats are arranged in rows with an equal number of seats in each row. Can you work out how many different ways the seats can be arranged? To do this you need to find the factors of 24.

Prime numbers

Toadie's favourite numbers are primes. These are numbers with only two factors, 1 and the number itself, like 17. A way of finding prime numbers was worked out over 2,000 years ago by an Ancient Greek, called Eratosthenes. Toadie explains what Eratosthenes did, below.

1 is not counted as a prime number.

Eratosthenes called his method a sieve because he sifted out all the unwanted numbers.

Eratosthenes made a grid with a hundred blocks, like this one. He coloured in all the multiples of 2 to 10, except blocks 2 and 3. The prime numbers were all the numbers left uncoloured at the end. Toadie has coloured in all the multiples of 2 and 3 on the grid above. Make a copy and finish it off.

Odd fact

1	2	3	4	5	6
7	8	9	10	11	12
13	14	15	16	17	18
19	20	21	22	23	24
25	26	27	28	29	30
31	32	33	34	35	36
37	38	39	40	41	42
43	44	45	46	47	48
49	50	51	52	53	54
55	56	57	58	59	60
61	62	63	64	65	66
67	68	69	70	71	72
73	74	75	76	77	78
79	80	81	82	83	84
85	86	87	88	89	90
91	92	93	94	95	96
97	98	99	100	101	102

Toadie has coloured in the prime numbers on a grid 6 blocks wide. See how most of them fall on numbers which are one more or one less than multiples of 6.

Square numbers

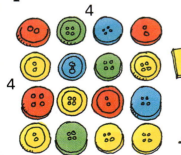

When you multiply a number by itself you get a square number. You can see why in this picture. Bigtum's brother has arranged his coat buttons in 4 rows of 4 to make a square of 16 buttons. So 16 is a square number.

$4 \times 4 = 16$

The number you divide by should equal the answer.

25 33
77 36 81
9 49 72

Are these numbers square numbers? Divide them on a calculator and see, but first take heed of the clue above.

Big sums

The quickest way to multiply and divide large numbers is on a calculator. But if you haven't got one handy, you can work them out on paper, just like you do with smaller numbers. The monster gang show you how quick and easy this way can be, too.

Multiplying

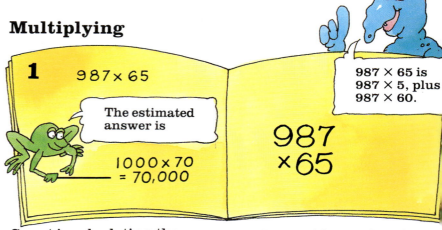

1 987 × 65

The estimated answer is 1000 × 70 = 70,000

987 × 65 is 987 × 5, plus 987 × 60.

987 ×65

Snout is calculating the number of kilotrotters* she has to run in the Monster Marathon. Each lap is 987 kilotrotters and there are 65 laps, so she needs to multiply 987 by 65. After estimating the answer, she sets the sum out in her notebook, but then gets stuck, so Toadie's friend explains how to do it, below.

2
```
   987
 × 65
  4935  (987×5)
```

First multiply 987 by 5, in the way shown on pages 14-15. That is, you multiply the units by 5, then the tens and finally the hundreds.

3
```
   987
 × 65
  4935  (987×5)
 59220  (987×60)
```

Next you multiply 987 × 6 in the same way, but first put a 0 in the units column. This is because you are multiplying by 6 tens.

4
```
    987
 ×   65
   4935  (987×5)
  59220  (987×60) +
  64155
```

64,155 is close to 70,000 so the answer is probably right.

Finally, add both parts of the sum together. This tells you what 987 × 65 is.

*1 kilotrotter = 1000 trotters.

Dividing

Toadie's bank manager, Grabber, is working out a complicated financial deal. It involves dividing 1193 by 37, so she has to calculate the 37s table. But first she works out an estimate. Can you work out the estimate for this sum?

Grabber then does the sum on a calculator to be extra accurate. She gets a recurring decimal, where the numbers after the decimal point repeat.

Puzzles

The biggest building in Monsterland has 44 storeys. Each storey is 579 trotters high. What is the height of the building?

Chief news reporter, Snout, types on average 45 words a minute. Today's article is 1485 words. How long did it take her to type?

Percentages

Percentages are special kinds of fractions. The number under the line is always 100. However, percentages are not written in the same way as ordinary fractions. Instead they are written as whole numbers, followed by the percentage sign, %. If you look carefully, you can see 1, 0 and 0 in the percentage sign.

Percentage comes from Latin words, *per centum*, which means "per 100".

Snout has planted 100 seeds in her garden and four different types have sprung up. The number of purple pansies has been written as a fraction and as a percentage. She wants to know what the others are as percentages, too.

How to work out percentages

20% of 54

$$54 \times \frac{20}{100} = \frac{1080}{100} = 10.8$$

To work out, say, 20% of 54, all you do is multiply 54 by $^{20}/_{100}$. Can you help Brumbleweed with his homework below?

Help!

35% of 56
40% of 82
33% of 43
21% of 77

On a calculator, you multiply the number by the percentage you want and press the % key.

Slimy Sid's stink bomb

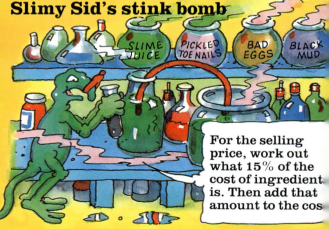

For the selling price, work out what 15% of the cost of ingredient is. Then add that amount to the cost

Slimy Sid makes giant stink bombs to sell to his friends. The ingredients for one stink bomb cost 18 munchies. He makes 15% profit on each one. How much is it to buy one of Slimy Sid's stink bombs?

Multiplying fractions

Multiplying fractions is quite easy, as Toadie shows.

$$\frac{1}{2} \times \frac{3}{5} = \frac{1 \times 3}{2 \times 5} = \frac{3}{10}$$

Toadie says to multiply two fractions, first multiply the tops together and then the bottoms.

$$\frac{3}{4} \times 60 = \frac{3}{4} \times \frac{60}{1} = \frac{3 \times 60}{4 \times 1} = \frac{180}{4} = 45$$

Multiplying fractions by whole numbers is just as simple. All you do is change the whole number into a fraction by putting it over 1. Then you multiply the two fractions together in the way shown above.

Making percentages

To turn a fraction into a percentage, all you do is multiply it by 100 as Toadie explains.

$$\frac{1}{2} \times \frac{100}{1} = \frac{100}{2} = 50\%$$

You can turn decimals into percentages, too. Just multiply them by 100.

$$0.35 \times 100 = 35\%$$

To turn a percentage into a fraction or decimal all you do is divide by 100.

$$9\% = \frac{9}{100} \text{ or } 0.09$$

Bigtum's bargain buy

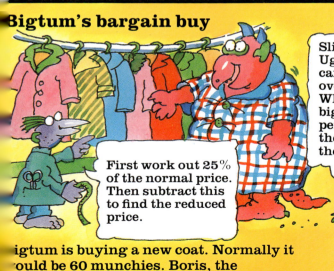

First work out 25% of the normal price. Then subtract this to find the reduced price.

Bigtum is buying a new coat. Normally it would be 60 munchies. Boris, the shopkeeper offers him 25% off because the coat belongs to last year's stock. How much will the coat cost after the reduction?

Which is bigger?

Slimy Sid and Ugly Mug can't agree over these. Which is bigger – the percentage or the fraction of these numbers?

64% of 60 OR $\frac{3}{4}$ of 60

8% of 45 OR $\frac{1}{6}$ of 45

72% of 34 OR $\frac{4}{5}$ of 34

Hints

When working out a fraction of a number, "of" means the same as "multiply by". For instance $\frac{2}{5}$ of 45 is the same as $\frac{2}{5} \times 45$.

$$\frac{2}{5} \text{ of } 45 = \frac{2}{5} \times 45$$
$$= \frac{2}{5} \times \frac{45}{1} = \frac{90}{5} = 18$$

Table tips

All the tables from 0 to 10 are shown below, in five different colours. If you learn a colour section at a time, there are less multiplications to remember. This is because multiplications repeat themselves (e.g. $3 \times 1 = 1 \times 3$). Follow the advice of Toby T. Table, on the right.

1 When you have learnt this section you know a third of your tables.

First learn the purple section. This contains all the sums in the 0 and 1s tables.

2 $2 \times 2 = 4$, $3 \times 2 = 6$. When you know the green sums too, you have learnt more than half your tables.

Next learn the green section. This covers the 2 and 10s tables.

```
0 × 0 = 0
0 × 1 = 0
0 × 2 = 0
0 × 3 = 0
0 × 4 = 0
0 × 5 = 0
0 × 6 = 0
0 × 7 = 0
0 × 8 = 0
0 × 9 = 0
0 × 10 = 0
```

A good way to learn is to chant the tables out loud.

```
1 × 0 = 0
1 × 1 = 1
1 × 2 = 2
1 × 3 = 3
1 × 4 = 4
1 × 5 = 5
1 × 6 = 6
1 × 7 = 7
1 × 8 = 8
1 × 9 = 9
1 × 10 = 10
```

```
2 × 0 = 0
2 × 1 = 2
2 × 2 = 4
2 × 3 = 6
2 × 4 = 8
2 × 5 = 10
2 × 6 = 12
2 × 7 = 14
2 × 8 = 16
2 × 9 = 18
2 × 10 = 20
```

```
6 × 0 = 0
6 × 1 = 6
6 × 2 = 12
6 × 3 = 18
6 × 4 = 24
6 × 5 = 30
6 × 6 = 36
6 × 7 = 42
6 × 8 = 48
6 × 9 = 54
6 × 10 = 60
```

```
7 × 0 = 0
7 × 1 = 7
7 × 2 = 14
7 × 3 = 21
7 × 4 = 28
7 × 5 = 35
7 × 6 = 42
7 × 7 = 49
7 × 8 = 56
7 × 9 = 63
7 × 10 = 70
```

When you think you know a whole table, get a friend to test you, or try writing it down from memory.

```
8 × 0 = 0
8 × 1 = 8
8 × 2 = 16
8 × 3 = 24
8 × 4 = 32
8 × 5 = 40
8 × 6 = 48
8 × 7 = 56
8 × 8 = 64
8 × 9 = 72
8 × 10 = 80
```

3

Now learn the red sums. Then you will know the 3 and the 5s tables.

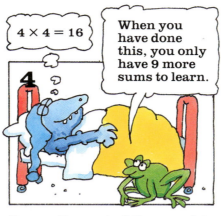

4

Learn the rest of the 4 and 6s tables, coloured blue.

5

Finally learn what is left of the 7, 8 and 9s tables.

3 × 0 = 0	4 × 0 = 0	5 × 0 = 0
3 × 1 = 3	4 × 1 = 4	5 × 1 = 5
3 × 2 = 6	4 × 2 = 8	5 × 2 = 10
3 × 3 = 9	4 × 3 = 12	5 × 3 = 15
3 × 4 = 12	4 × 4 = 16	5 × 4 = 20
3 × 5 = 15	4 × 5 = 20	5 × 5 = 25
3 × 6 = 18	4 × 6 = 24	5 × 6 = 30
3 × 7 = 21	4 × 7 = 28	5 × 7 = 35
3 × 8 = 24	4 × 8 = 32	5 × 8 = 40
3 × 9 = 27	4 × 9 = 36	5 × 9 = 45
3 × 10 = 30	4 × 10 = 40	5 × 10 = 50

Look, the answers to the 5s table always end in 0 or 5.

9 × 0 = 0	10 × 0 = 0
9 × 1 = 9	10 × 1 = 10
9 × 2 = 18	10 × 2 = 20
9 × 3 = 27	10 × 3 = 30
9 × 4 = 36	10 × 4 = 40
9 × 5 = 45	10 × 5 = 50
9 × 6 = 54	10 × 6 = 60
9 × 7 = 63	10 × 7 = 70
9 × 8 = 72	10 × 8 = 80
9 × 9 = 81	10 × 9 = 90
9 × 10 = 90	10 × 10 = 100

If you add the two figures in the answers to this table they always add up to 9. Try them and see.

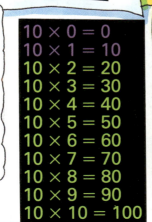

Over the page there is a computer game to help you practise your tables.

Treasure hunt

If you have a computer or can borrow one, you can type in and play this simple game.

You have to find hoards of treasure, each one guarded by a bull. At each stage, the computer asks you a tables question. If you are wrong you go back a stage. When you have all the treasure, the computer gives you a score.

Before you start, read the hints on the opposite page.

*This program works on the Commodore 64, Vic 20, Apple, TRS-80 COL 32K, BBC, Electron, Spectrum and MSX.

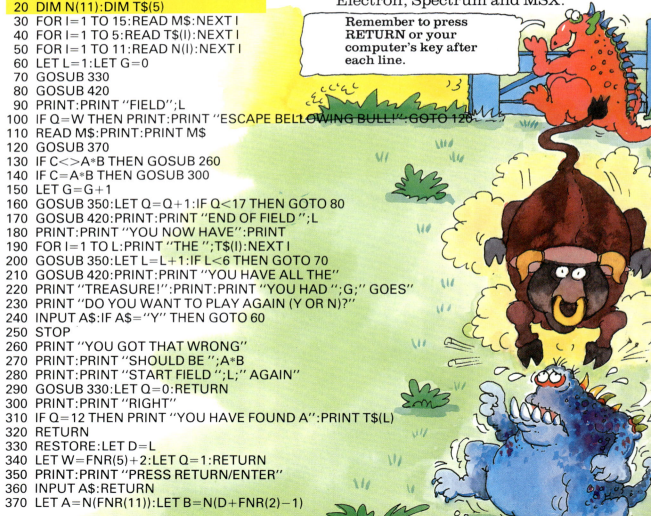

Remember to press RETURN or your computer's key after each line.

```
10   DEF FNR(X)=INT(RND(1)*X+1)
20   DIM N(11):DIM T$(5)
30   FOR I=1 TO 15:READ M$:NEXT I
40   FOR I=1 TO 5:READ T$(I):NEXT I
50   FOR I=1 TO 11:READ N(I):NEXT I
60   LET L=1:LET G=0
70   GOSUB 330
80   GOSUB 420
90   PRINT:PRINT "FIELD";L
100  IF Q=W THEN PRINT:PRINT "ESCAPE BELLOWING BULL!":GOTO 120
110  READ M$:PRINT:PRINT M$
120  GOSUB 370
130  IF C<>A*B THEN GOSUB 260
140  IF C=A*B THEN GOSUB 300
150  LET G=G+1
160  GOSUB 350:LET Q=Q+1:IF Q<17 THEN GOTO 80
170  GOSUB 420:PRINT:PRINT "END OF FIELD ";L
180  PRINT:PRINT "YOU NOW HAVE":PRINT
190  FOR I=1 TO L:PRINT "THE ";T$(I):NEXT I
200  GOSUB 350:LET L=L+1:IF L<6 THEN GOTO 70
210  GOSUB 420:PRINT:PRINT "YOU HAVE ALL THE"
220  PRINT "TREASURE!":PRINT:PRINT "YOU HAD ";G;" GOES"
230  PRINT "DO YOU WANT TO PLAY AGAIN (Y OR N)?"
240  INPUT A$:IF A$="Y" THEN GOTO 60
250  STOP
260  PRINT "YOU GOT THAT WRONG"
270  PRINT:PRINT "SHOULD BE ";A*B
280  PRINT:PRINT "START FIELD ";L;" AGAIN"
290  GOSUB 330:LET Q=0:RETURN
300  PRINT:PRINT "RIGHT"
310  IF Q=12 THEN PRINT "YOU HAVE FOUND A":PRINT T$(L)
320  RETURN
330  RESTORE:LET D=L
340  LET W=FNR(5)+2:LET Q=1:RETURN
350  PRINT:PRINT "PRESS RETURN/ENTER"
360  INPUT A$:RETURN
370  LET A=N(FNR(11)):LET B=N(D+FNR(2)−1)
```

```
380 PRINT:PRINT "WHAT IS      ";A;" X ";B
390 INPUT C
400 IF D<L+5 THEN LET D=D+1
410 RETURN
420 CLS
430 PRINT:PRINT " TREASURE HUNT ":RETURN
440 DATA "OVER THE GATE"
450 DATA "MIDDLE OF THE FIELD"
460 DATA "WALK NORTH", "WALK WEST"
470 DATA "WALK SOUTH", "WALK NORTH"
480 DATA "WALK EAST", "CHOP DOWN THE TREE"
490 DATA "DIG UP THE ROOTS"
500 DATA "ROLL AWAY THE BOULDER"
510 DATA "BREAK OPEN THE CHEST"
520 DATA "TAKE THE TREASURE"
530 DATA "CLIMB OUT OF THE HOLE"
540 DATA "ESCAPE CHARGING BULL!"
550 DATA "JUMP OVER THE GATE"
560 DATA "HUGE JAR OF GOLD MUNCHIES"
570 DATA "BAG OF GIANT JUMPING BEANS"
580 DATA "MONSTER BOX OF CHOX"
590 DATA "BARREL OF HEADCASES'S PARTY JUICE"
600 DATA "PAIR OF MAGIC WINGS"
610 DATA 0,1,2,10,3,5,6,4,7,8,9
```

Each time you play the game see if you can improve your score.

Typing in the program hints

Type in each line exactly as it is printed. When you come to a line on a yellow stripe, look under the name of your computer on the right. If there is a line with the same number as the one on the stripe, type it in instead of the one on the stripe.

Spectrum	10 DEF FN R(X) = INT(RND*X+1) 20 DIM N(11):DIM T$(5,31)
Vic 20/Commodore 64	420 PRINT CHR$(147)
TRS-80 COL 32K	10 DEF FNR(X) = INT(RND(0)*X+1)
Apple	420 HOME

Ten times  If you add this line to the program, you can practise multiplying by tens, too.

375 IF FNR(10)<2 THEN LET A = A*10

Answers

Page 2
1. $5 \times 2 = 10$
2. $4 \times 2 = 8$
3. $4 \times 3 = 12$

Page 3
Bigtum's shopping expedition

$8 \times 2 = 16$ monstermallows
$6 \times 3 = 18$ orangofruits
$7 \times 5 = 35$ snappercrackers
$9 \times 2 = 18$ monsterchox

Using multiplication

A quick way is to multiply 4 by 8.
$4 \times 8 = 32$, so Aunty Mabel needs 32 munchies.

Pages 4-5
Hops and jumps

After 4 hops Toadie lands on 16, so $4 \times 4 = 16$.

Leap frog

1. $2 \times 3 = 6$
2. $2 \times 4 = 8$ $\quad 2 \times 5 = 10$
   $2 \times 6 = 12$
3. $3\frac{1}{2} \times 2 = 7$ $\quad 3\frac{1}{2} \times 3 = 10\frac{1}{2}$
4. 0 3 6 9 12 15 <u>18</u>

   0 7 <u>14</u>

   0 4 8 12 <u>16</u> <u>20</u>

Stepping stones

They can jump in 7s or 8s.

Which way round

$2 \times 6 = 12$
$6 \times 2 = 12$

Page 6
Bigtum's monster cake

$5 \times 4 = 20$ squirts of greasy goo
$8 \times 4 = 32$ blobs of pink puffs
$6 \times 4 = 24$ blobs of crazy crunch
$2 \times 4 = 8$ dinosaur eggs
$7 \times 4 = 28$ blobs of sherbert fizz
$10 \times 4 = 40$ chocolate bubbles
$4 \times 4 = 16$ squirts of cream

How heavy is Ugly Mug?

$5 \times 9 = 45$ kiloblobs

Party puzzle

$7 \times 6 = 42$ bottles

Page 8
3. You get a five point star.
4. You get a five point star if you jump in 2s and a pentagon if you jump in 4s or 6s.
5. The 3s or the 5s table.

Page 9
Tens puzzle

$40 \times 2 = 80$ trotters long

Page 10
1. $8 \div 2 = 4$ bones each
2. $9 \div 3 = 3$ sticks each
3. $20 \div 5 = 4$ seeds in each pot

Page 11
Headcase and the chocobars

$12 \div 4 = 3$
There are 3 groups of 4.
$10 \div 2 = 5$
$21 \div 7 = 3$
$30 \div 3 = 10$
$24 \div 4 = 6$

Hopping backwards

It takes 7 hops of 2 to get back to 0.
$16 \div 4 = 4$
$20 \div 5 = 4$
$15 \div 3 = 5$

Page 12
Left overs

$36 \div 5 = 7$ remainder 1
$84 \div 9 = 9$ remainder 3
$42 \div 7 = 6$
$55 \div 6 = 9$ remainder 1
$28 \div 3 = 9$ remainder 1

Brain teaser

$36 \div 6 = 6$
$36 \div 7 = 5$ remainder 1
$36 \div 4 = 9$
$36 \div 5 = 7$ remainder 1

The answer could be 7 or 5.

Page 13
One more cake
The two left over cakes could be cut up in any of these 3 ways, so each monster gets ⅔ each.

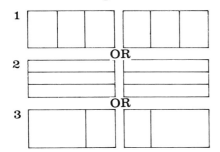

Monsterous problems
1. 39 ÷ 7 = 5 remainder 4
2. 13 ÷ 2 = 6½ trotters
3. 49 ÷ 5 = 9⅘ seconds

Page 15
Headcase's holiday puzzle
Headcase has to wait 27 monster weeks and Slimy Sid has to wait 77 days.

Page 16
Aunty Mabel's knitting
44 ÷ 5 = 8.8 trotters.

Page 17
Grumble's bubble gum
1.5 × 9 = 13.5 munchies

Ugly Mug's matching game
3.6 × 5 = 18
43.1 × 7 = 301.7
41 ÷ 8 = 5.125
17 ÷ 4 = 4.25
54 ÷ 0.3 = 180
74 ÷ 2.5 = 29.6

Page 18
Checking the answer
42 × 5 = 210
770 ÷ 8 = 96.25
1870 × 9 = 16830

Estimates
40 × 5 = 200
800 ÷ 8 = 100
2000 × 9 = 18000

Try these
67 ÷ 2 = 33.5
143 ÷ 5 = 28.6
3726 ÷ 9 = 414
53 × 9 = 477
276 × 7 = 1932
1250 × 4 = 5000

Estimates
70 ÷ 2 = 35
100 ÷ 5 = 20
4000 ÷ 10 = 400
50 × 10 = 500
300 × 7 = 2100
1000 × 4 = 4000

Page 19
Games and guesses
1. 720 is the biggest and the smallest number.
2. 542 ÷ 2 = 271
   923 × 6 = 5538
   3.52 × 8 = 28.16
   987 ÷ 3 = 329
   654 ÷ 8 = 81.75

Page 20
Special numbers
8 and 1 are also factors of 8.

Monstermobile route numbers
The factors of
18 are 1,2,3,6,9,18
27 are 1,3,9,27
42 are 1,2,3,6,7,14,21,42
64 are 1,2,4,8,16,32,64
72 are 1,2,3,4,6,8,9,18, 24,36,72
89 are 1,89
55 are 1,5,11,55

True or false?
Headcase and Snout.

Monstermobile bus
1 row of 24 seats
24 rows of 1 seats
2 rows of 12 seats
12 rows of 2 seats
3 rows of 8 seats
8 rows of 3 seats
4 rows of 6 seats
6 rows of 4 seats

Page 21
Square numbers
3 × 3 = 9
5 × 5 = 25
6 × 6 = 36
7 × 7 = 49
9 × 9 = 81

Page 23
Dividing
The estimate is 1200 ÷ 40 = 30
Puzzles
1
```
    579
×    44
   2316
  23160
  —————
  25476
```

The building is 25476 trotters high.

Answers

Page 23

2.
```
        30+3
   45|1485
     -1350   (45×30)
      ────
       135
      -135   (45×3)
      ────
       000
```

Snout took 33 minutes to type the article.

Page 24-25
Percentages
Blue bloomers 9%
Pink pongs 31%
Scarlet stinkers 13%

How to work out percentages

35% of $56 = 56 \times \frac{35}{100}$

$= \frac{1960}{100} = 19.6\%$

40% of $82 = 82 \times \frac{40}{100}$

$= \frac{3280}{100} = 32.8\%$

33% of $43 = 43 \times \frac{33}{100}$

$= \frac{1419}{100} = 14.19\%$

21% of $77 = 77 \times \frac{21}{100}$

$= \frac{1617}{100} = 16.17\%$

Slimy Sid's stink bomb
15% of $18 = 2.7$
$18 + 2.7 = 20.7$ munchies

Bigtum's bargain coat
25% of $60 = 15$
$60 - 15 = 45$ munchies

Which is bigger
64% of $60 = 38.4$
$¾$ of $60 = 45$
72% of $34 = 24.48$
$⅘$ of $34 = 27.2$
8% of $45 = 3.6$
$⅙$ of $45 = 7.5$

So all the fractions are bigger

Toby's table square

One of Toby T. Table's specialities is his table square. It contains the multiples of all the tables and is very useful for quickly checking the answers to problems.

For instance, to find out 8×9, you look along row 8, until you meet column 9 and there you find the answer, 72.

You can use it for division, too. To check what, say, $42 \div 7$ is, look down column 7 until you come to 42. Then look to see what row 42 is in and you find the answer 6.

Columns →

×	0	1	2	3	4	5	6	7	8	9	10
0	0	0	0	0	0	0	0	0	0	0	0
1	0	1	2	3	4	5	6	7	8	9	10
2	0	2	4	6	8	10	12	14	16	18	20
3	0	3	6	9	12	15	18	21	24	27	30
4	0	4	8	12	16	20	24	28	32	36	40
5	0	5	10	15	20	25	30	35	40	45	50
6	0	6	12	18	24	30	36	42	48	54	60
7	0	7	14	21	28	35	42	49	56	63	70
8	0	8	16	24	32	40	48	56	64	72	80
9	0	9	18	27	36	45	54	63	72	81	90
10	0	10	20	30	40	50	60	70	80	90	100

Rows

WEIGHING & MEASURING

Contents

- 36 Body measurements
- 38 Little lengths
- 40 Big distances
- 42 Weight and weightlessness
- 44 Kilos, pounds and blobs
- 46 Weighing machines
- 48 Hot and cold
- 50 Measuring area
- 52 Special shapes
- 54 Cubes
- 56 Measuring liquids
- 58 Slopes and corners
- 60 Measures chart
- 62 Puzzle answers
- 64 Index

About this section

In this section the Monster Gang shows you how to measure things such as length, weight, and temperature. There are two main systems of measuring, Metric and Imperial. Nowadays most countries use the Metric system which was first developed in France. The Imperial system was developed in Britain and is still used in America. However, U.S. pints and gallons are slightly smaller than the old Imperial pints and gallons.

On pages 60-61 there is a measures chart. You can use it to compare Metric and Imperial measures.

Different kinds of measuring

1 The next few pages are all about measuring length, height and distance. The Monster Gang explains what kind of measuring instruments you can use.

2 Then Bigtum and Gong explain weight – what it is and how to measure it. You can find out how to make your own weighing-scales.

3 On pages 48-49 the monsters investigate temperature. They tell you all about the different temperature scales and some fun facts about temperature.

4 You can also find out how to calculate the surface of an object, called its area. Snout tells you about rules for finding the area of special shapes, too.

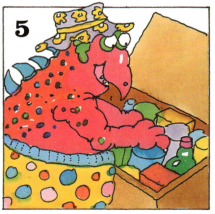

5 The amount of space an object takes up is called its volume. The Monster Gang shows you how to work out the volume of solid objects and liquids.

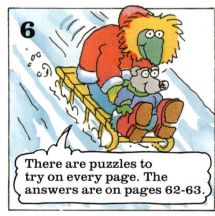

6 There are puzzles to try on every page. The answers are on pages 62-63.

On pages 58-59 Dodo and Dogosaurus help you discover how to measure the steepness of a slope. Toadie explains how to measure the sharpness of a corner.

Body measurements

Professor Toga, the monster historian, is explaining how people once used parts of their bodies to measure things.

The Ancient Romans used their feet to measure distances. For small lengths they used a thumb width, called an uncia.

They measured longer distances in paces. A pace was two steps: one with the left foot and one with the right. For very big distances the Romans used miles. A mile was then the distance of 1000 paces. The word mile comes from a Latin word, *mille*, which means 1000.

Feet and thumbs

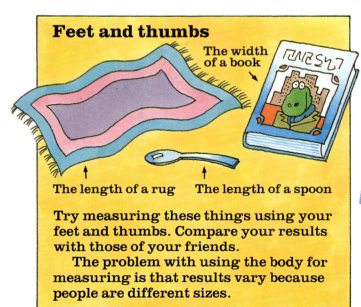

Try measuring these things using your feet and thumbs. Compare your results with those of your friends.

The problem with using the body for measuring is that results vary because people are different sizes.

A standard measure

Miles, yards, feet and inches became known as the Imperial system of measuring.

The English king, Henry 1 (1068-1135), introduced a measure that would be the same for everyone. It was the distance from his nose to his thumb, called a yard. Feet and inches then became fixed measures, too.

Metric measuring

Many countries today use a standard measure called a metre, which is just bigger than a yard. The metre is part of an international system of measuring, called the Metric system. The metre of cloth Fancy buys in France is the same length as the metre of wire Goofy buys in Australia.

Un mètre s'il vous plaît.

One metre, please, cobber.

Which measuring system do you use, Metric or Imperial?

The Metric system uses kilometres for very big distances and centimetres and millimetres for small lengths.

Measures then and now

Roman
1 mile = 1000 paces
1 pace = 5 feet
1 foot = 12 uncia

Metric
1 kilometre = 1000 metres
1 metre = 100 centimetres
1 centimetre = 10 millimetres

Imperial
1 mile = 1760 yards
1 yard = 3 feet
1 foot = 12 inches

A kilometre is just a bit further than half a mile.

Toga's measuring puzzle

Below there are some common measures. Which type would you use to measure the things in the picture?

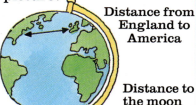

Distance from England to America

Distance to the moon

Depth of snow on the ground

A length of dress material

The size of a shirt collar

KILOMETRES / MILES

METRES / YARDS

CENTIMETRES / INCHES

Little lengths

Nowadays people use rulers and tape-measures to measure short lengths. Metric rulers and tape-measures are marked with centimetres. Each centimetre is divided into ten parts, called millimetres.

This monterosa flower is 90cm high. How many millimetres is that?

You will need a ruler or tape-measure to do the puzzle below.

Don't believe your eyes!

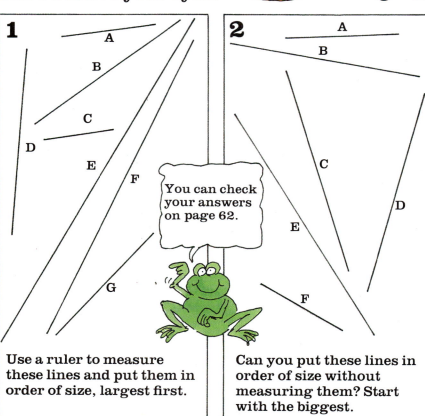

You can check your answers on page 62.

1 Use a ruler to measure these lines and put them in order of size, largest first.

2 Can you put these lines in order of size without measuring them? Start with the biggest.

3 Which of these matchsticks do you think is longest? Beware, your eyes may deceive you!

Check your answer by measuring them.

38

Monster measures

The monsters have their own measuring system called Monsterics. Their rulers and tape-measures are divided into make-believe lengths called trotters. A trotter is about the length of a monster's foot.

Gong and Hattie are guessing the lengths of things and checking their guesses with a

Guess and measure

The distance round your head

The length of your legs

The width of a window

tape-measure. Try playing this game with a friend and see whose guesses are closer.*

Hattie's jellybean burger

This is Hattie's mid-morning jellybean burger. The measurements of the ingredients are shown in the picture. How tall is Hattie's burger?

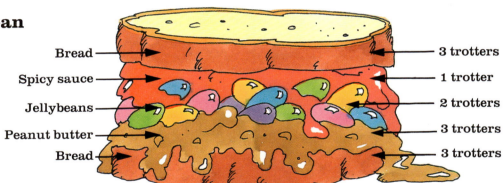

- Bread — 3 trotters
- Spicy sauce — 1 trotter
- Jellybeans — 2 trotters
- Peanut butter — 3 trotters
- Bread — 3 trotters

Did you know?

To begin with the length of a metre was based on the distance between two places. Surveyors in France worked out the length of a line from the North pole to the Equator, through Paris. They divided it into ten million parts and called each part a metre.

Scientists have now found a very accurate way to define the metre, using light.

*Use a Metric ruler or tape-measure.

Big distances

Some distances are too big to measure with a ruler. For measuring things like the length of your garden or the distance from one town to another, you need special equipment.

You could use a yard trundle wheel to measure the plot in yards.

Trundle wheel — 1 metre

Snout is using a special wheel called a trundle wheel to measure her vegetable plot. Each time the wheel rotates it clicks. On Snout's wheel one rotation is equal to a metre, so by counting the clicks she can measure the edges of the plot in metres.

Trundle puzzle

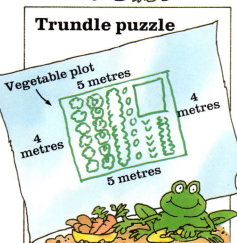

Vegetable plot — 5 metres, 4 metres, 4 metres, 5 metres

Can you work out how many times Snout's trundle wheel rotated when she was measuring out her vegetable plot?

Long distance

The distance travelled is displayed in a panel on the dashboard.

Odometer 245

This monstermobile has travelled 245 kilometres.

An odometer is an instrument attached to the wheel of a vehicle. It records the distance it has travelled.

Matching puzzle

Building site worker
Lorry driver
Odometer — 245
Decorator
Tape-measure
Trundle wheel
Ruler
Dressmaker

Can you match these measuring instruments with their owners?

How far is it?

This triangular chart shows the distances between towns in Monsterland. To find the distance between two places, move your finger across from one place and up from the other. The square where they meet shows the distance between them.

The distances on this chart are in kilotrotters.*

Trumpington	141	81	134	114	78	91	58	78	144	162
Honkery		182	263	128	103	51	199	175	271	21
Nottyville			177	94	151	157	50	155	183	204
Trottersfield				248	161	213	128	92	54	284
Scaleswell					154	107	127	191	260	133
Hump Norton						52	135	73	191	124
Bogchester							148	125	220	72
Slimepool								106	133	220
Sludgemouth									123	197
Wastewater										292

The Monster Department of the Environment need to know the answers to these questions. Can you help?

1. How far is it from Trumpington to Hump Norton?
2. How far is it from Nottyville to Slimepool?
3. Which is nearer to Trottersfield, Bogchester or Trumpington?

Monsterous mountains

Hovel Heights — 483 trotters
Fungus Tip — 1304 trotters
Pong Point — 2046 trotters
Putrid Peak — 742 trotters

The monster climbing team are on an expedition. The heights of the peaks they aim to conquer are shown above.

*A kilotrotter is 1000 trotters.

Mountain quiz

1. Can you put the peaks in order of height, highest first?
2. What is the difference in height between the highest and the lowest mountain?
3. Which two mountains, on top of each other, would equal the height of the highest mountain?

Weight

The weight of an object depends on both its size and what it is made of. Bigtum and Gong have discovered that a tiny piece of lead weighs the same as a huge bag of feathers. This is because lead is a heavy material.

Can you think of any other very heavy materials?

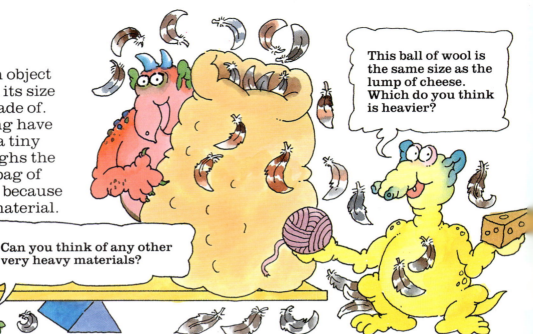

This ball of wool is the same size as the lump of cheese. Which do you think is heavier?

What is weight?

Toothpeg says try holding a bag of sugar in your outstretched hand for a while. Although its weight does not change, it seems to get heavier as your arm tires.

Weight pulling down

Arm pushing up

The weight of the sugar is like a force, pulling it towards the ground. To support it, you have to push back with a force of your own, which makes your arm tired.

Supporting your weight

Your bones and muscles are designed to support your weight. Try this experiment and see.

Sit in a chair, with your feet on the ground. Then stand up without moving your feet. Can you feel your leg muscles pushing down on the floor in order to support your weight?

When you swim, the water helps to support your weight, so you feel lighter. A whale would collapse on land because it needs water to help support its weight.

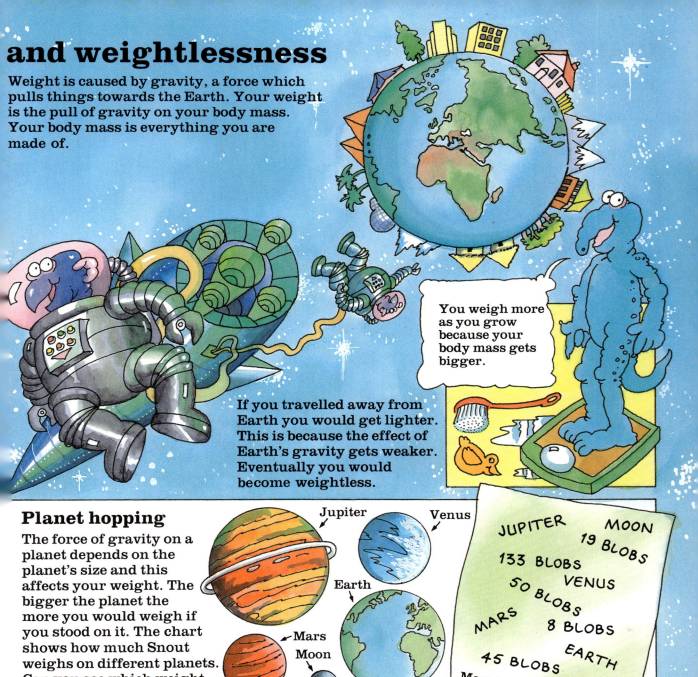

Kilos, pounds and blobs

The Monsteric system of measuring uses units called blobs for weighing things. However, when Bigtum is asked to judge an international cookery competition he needs to know about Imperial and Metric weights, too.

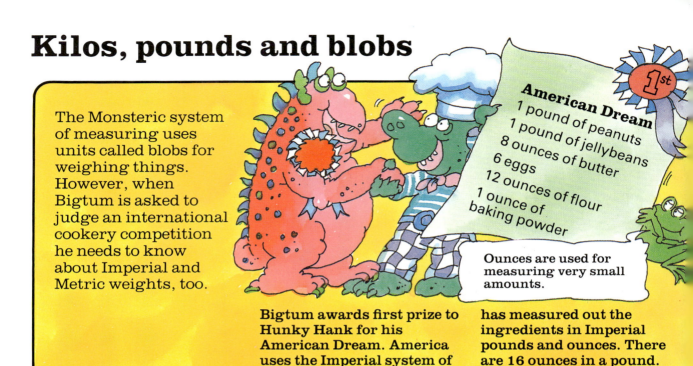

American Dream
1 pound of peanuts
1 pound of jellybeans
8 ounces of butter
6 eggs
12 ounces of flour
1 ounce of baking powder

Ounces are used for measuring very small amounts.

Bigtum awards first prize to Hunky Hank for his American Dream. America uses the Imperial system of measuring, so Hunky Hank has measured out the ingredients in Imperial pounds and ounces. There are 16 ounces in a pound.

Gong's experiment

Gong has listed some things for you to weigh. You can use any type of kitchen scales. Before you weigh them hold each object in your hand and see if you can put them in order of weight, heaviest first. Then record their exact weights. Did you guess the right order?

Slimy Sid's trick

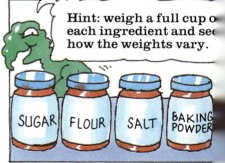

Hint: weigh a full cup of each ingredient and see how the weights vary.

Slimy Sid has swapped over Aunty Mabel's jar labels. She keeps the jars full and in order of weight, the heaviest on the right. In what order should the labels be?

Super Snail Surprise
750 grams of snails
500 grams of garlic
2 kilograms of cheese
1 kilogram of chopped onions
1 kilogram of butter

1 kilogram is equal to 2.2 pounds.

He awards second prize to France's Ghastly Gaston for his Super Snail Surprise. Gaston has measured out his ingredients in Metric measures – grams and kilograms. There are **1000** grams in a kilogram. One gram is a very, very tiny amount.

International weight chart

The letters in brackets are short for each measure.

Metric
1000 grams (g) = 1 kilogram (kg)

The word ounce, like inch, comes from the Latin word, *uncia*.

Imperial
16 ounces (oz) = 1 pound (lb)

Weighing yourself

How much do you weigh?

Most countries use kilograms or pounds to record a person's weight. In Great Britain people often weigh themselves in stones. (A stone is 14 pounds.)

Amazing weights

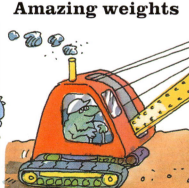

The heaviest recorded man was an American, R.E. Hughes. When he died in 1958, he weighed 485kg. His coffin was a crate which was lowered by a crane.

The thinnest person of normal height was an American woman. She weighed 22kg – about the same weight as Hughes' head.

Weighing machines

Gong and his team are discovering ways to measure weight. A simple way is to balance the object you want to weigh against a known weight. To do this you need a balance "scale" like the one shown on the right.

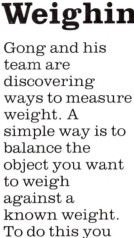

Some balance scales have hanging pans like this one.

A balance scale has two sides. When both are empty they balance. If you put an object on one side, that side goes down because it is now heavier than the other side.

To find out how heavy the object is you put known weights on the empty side until the two sides balance again. How much does Toadie weigh?

Toothpeg's puzzle

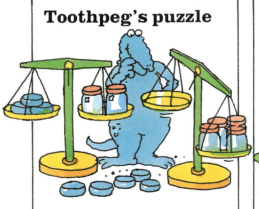

Toothpeg is weighing marmalade jars using blob weights. How many blobs will make the righthand scales balance?

Spring scales

Pointer

Weight can stretch or squash a spring. On this spring scale a pointer indicates the weight as the spring stretches.

Bigtum's balance

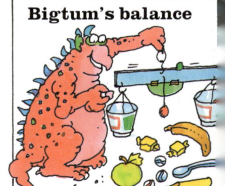

Opposite you can find out how to make a balance like Bigtum's. You can use it to compare the weights of different objects.

Making a balance scale

Things you need

A piece of thick cardboard about 60cm long and 2.5cm wide, with holes at either end and in the middle.

Two identical yoghurt pots (large ones are best), each with two holes bored directly opposite each other just below the rim.

Three large paper-clips

Plasticine and string

A piece of thin card about 15cm square

A ruler and pencil

A saucer for drawing a circle

Sticky tape and a drawing pin

Before you start get a grown-up to make the holes in the cardboard and yoghurt pots using sharp scissors.

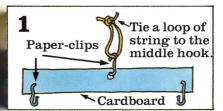

1 Tie a loop of string to the middle hook. Paper-clips. Cardboard.

Unbend one end of the three paper-clips and push them through the holes in the cardboard strip to make hooks.

2 This line must be directly below the hole.

On thin card draw a circle and divide it into quarters. Cut the circle in half and tape one half to the centre of the cardboard strip.*

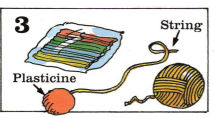

3 String. Plasticine.

Cut a piece of string about 15cm long, tie a knot in one end and wrap a ball of plasticine round it to make a weight.

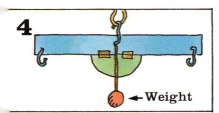

4 Weight

Fix the weight to the cardboard strip by threading the string through the middle hole and knotting it at the back.

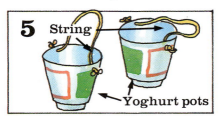

5 String. Yoghurt pots.

Knot strings about 50cm long through the holes in each pot and hang the pots on the hooks at either end of the balance.

6 Make sure the balance hangs freely.

Pin the balance up. If it tilts stick a small lump of plasticine on the lighter side and move it along until the two sides balance.

*You don't need the other half of the circle.

Hot and cold

A scale of 0 to 100 is usually used to measure heat. This scale is called centigrade, which means "100 steps", or degrees. A degree is shown with the symbol, °. Sometimes the scale is called Celsius, after the Swedish astronomer who invented it in 1742.

On Celsius' scale water freezes at 0°C and boils at 100°C.

In America a scale named after a man called Fahrenheit is used to measure temperature. Fahrenheit's scale is often used in Great Britain, too.

On Fahrenheit's scale water freezes at 32°F and boils at 212°F.

An instrument for measuring temperature is called a thermometer. You can see one in the picture on the right. Thermometers contain the liquid metal, mercury, which expands quickly when it gets hot. When the temperature rises, the level of the mercury in the thermometer rises, too.

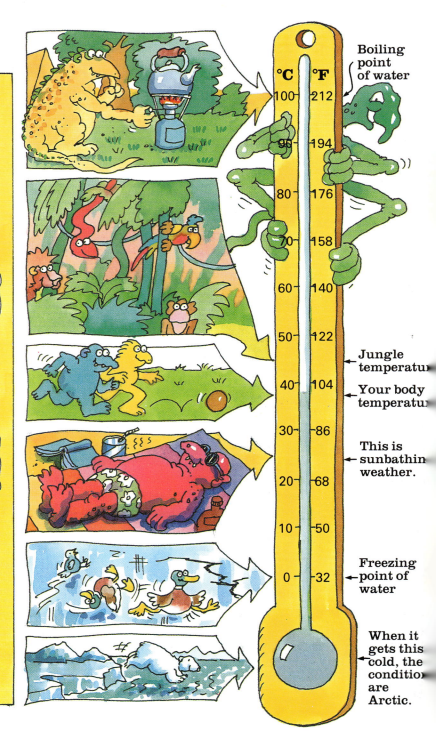

Boiling and freezing

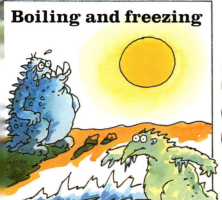

The temperature of the sun's surface is 6,000°C or 10,832°F. The lowest temperature possible is believed to be −273°C or −523.4°F. Then even the air would be frozen.

Ill?

Hint: a monster's normal temperature is the same as a human's – 37°C or 98.6°F.

Slimy Sid is pretending he's ill so he doesn't have to do the washing up. Aunty Mabel takes his temperature but when her back is turned, Slimy Sid puts the thermometer in a cup of hot lemon ooze. When Aunty Mabel looks at the thermometer, Slimy Sid's temperature is 3 times what it should be. How hot is the ooze?

Monster weather

Plodsedge 16°C
Slimepool 18°C
Hump Norton 21°C
Puddlepoint 10°C
Trumpington Lake 0°C
Bogchester 7°C

Dodo and Dogosaurus are planning a grand tour of Slime Island. They need to know what clothes to pack. Here is a weather map showing the temperatures they can expect in different places. Can you help Dodo and Dogosaurus find out the answers to the following questions?

1. Which town will have the highest temperature?
2. Which town will be the coldest?
3. Which seaside resort looks best for sunbathing?
4. Where will be the best place for ice skating?
5. What will be the difference in temperature between Plodsedge and Puddlepoint?

Measuring area

Measuring the size of a surface, such as a table top or baking tray, is called measuring an area. Bigtum and Hattie want to measure the area of a baking tray. They decide to cover it with cakes and count how many will fit on.

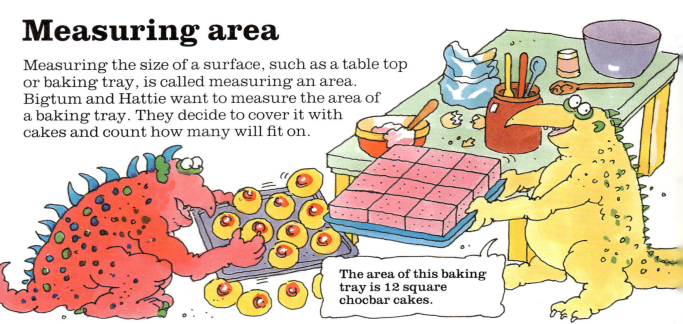

The area of this baking tray is 12 square chocbar cakes.

Bigtum has made round jumjubby cakes. Whichever way he arranges them on the tray there are gaps. Round shapes are not very good for measuring an area because they do not cover the surface completely.

Hattie has made square chocbar cakes. They cover the whole tray with no gaps. So Hattie can measure the area of the baking tray in square chocbar cakes.

Little and large

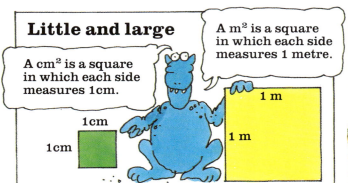

A cm² is a square in which each side measures 1cm.

A m² is a square in which each side measures 1 metre.

Squares are the best shape for measuring area because they fit together easily. In real life we use square centimetres (cm² for short), and so on to measure area.

The size of squares you use depends on how big an area you want to measure. Which of the measurements on Grumble's paper would you use to measure the area of these things?

*A hectare is a square with sides measuring 100 metres and an acre is a square with sides measuring 69.5 yards.

Rectangle puzzle

Snout's way

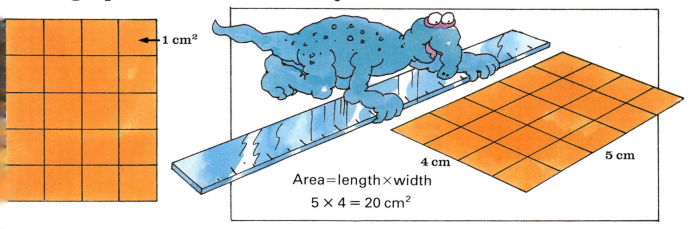

What is the area of this rectangle? You can find out by counting how many square centimetres there are.

Snout knows a quick way to work out the area of a rectangle. She measures the sides with a ruler and then multiplies the length by the width. The rectangle is 4 cm wide and 5 cm long, so its area is 20 cm².

Area = length × width
5 × 4 = 20 cm²

Try these

7 m / 4 m

2 m / 5 m

3 m / 3 m

You can work out the area of any rectangle or square by multiplying the width by the length. Try these.

Wiggly shapes

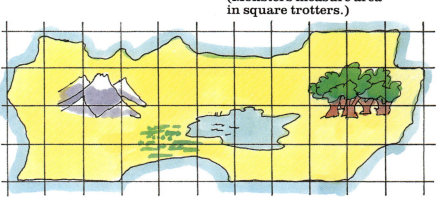

Each square represents a square trotter. (Monsters measure area in square trotters.)

Finding the area of wiggly shapes, like Slime Island is more tricky. First you count how many whole squares there are. Then you have to piece together the bits round the edge and see how many whole squares they make. Can you work out the area of Slime Island?

Special shapes

On the previous page Snout showed how to find the area of a rectangle or square by multiplying its length by its width. You can use Snout's rule for finding the area of other shapes too.

1 Triangles

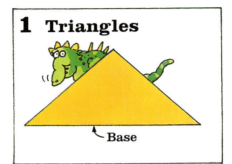

Grumble is wondering how to find the area of a triangle. A triangle is a shape which has three sides. Its bottom is called the base.

2

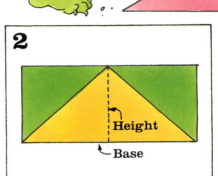

If you draw a rectangle which has the same base and height as the triangle, the area of the rectangle is twice the area of the triangle.

3

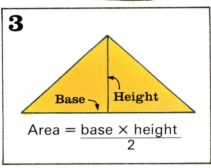

$$\text{Area} = \frac{\text{base} \times \text{height}}{2}$$

To find the area of the triangle you work out the area of the rectangle (base × height) and then divide it in half.

Monster modern art

Dodo is painting a portrait of Dogosaurus. The measurements (in trotters) are shown on the right. Dodo has one tin of paint which will cover an area of 40 square trotters. Is that enough to paint the portrait?

Hint: you need to work out the area of each part of Dogosaurus and then add the parts together.

Portrait measurements

EARS	HEIGHT = 2 BASE = 1
HEAD	WIDTH = 3 LENGTH = 5
BODY	BASE = 6 HEIGHT = 10
TAIL	WIDTH = 1 LENGTH = 2

Circles

A circle only has one edge. The distance round the edge is called the circumference and the distance from the middle to the edge is called the radius.

To find out the area of a circle imagine cutting it into lots of little pieces as shown below.

Then arrange the pieces side by side, half with their points up and half with their points down to make a rectangle.

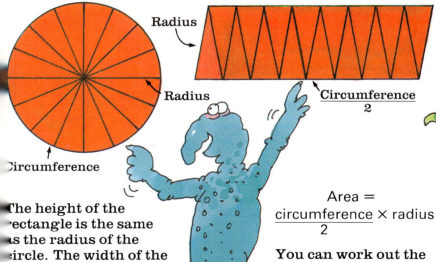

The height of the rectangle is the same as the radius of the circle. The width of the rectangle is equal to half the distance round the circumference.

$$\text{Area} = \frac{\text{circumference}}{2} \times \text{radius}$$

You can work out the area of the circle by multiplying half the circumference by the radius.

Grumble's new house

Grumble is moving house. He is not sure whether his furniture will fit in his new living room. Can you help him by working out how much space each piece of furniture takes up? The measurements of the furniture are shown (in trotters) at the bottom of the page.

Cubes

The amount of space an object fills is called its volume. To measure volume you use blocks called cubes. A block in which all the sides measure a metre is called a cubic metre. A block in which all the sides measure 1 centimetre is called a cubic centimetre.

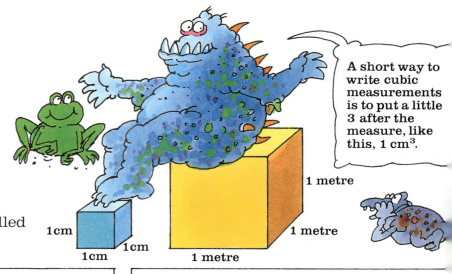

A short way to write cubic measurements is to put a little 3 after the measure, like this, 1 cm³.

1 Measuring volume

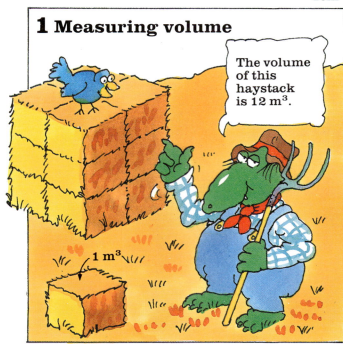

The volume of this haystack is 12 m³.

Turniptoes is making a haystack. Each bale of hay measures 1 cubic metre (1 m³), so he can work out the volume of the haystack by counting how many bales there are. Has he got the right answer?

2

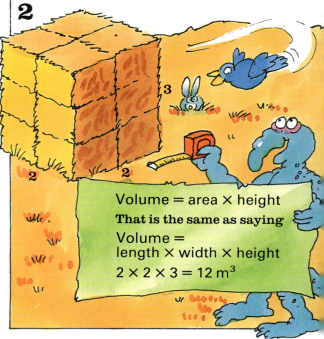

Volume = area × height

That is the same as saying

Volume = length × width × height

2 × 2 × 3 = 12 m³

Snout knows another way to work out volumes. You measure the width and length and work out the area the object covers. Then you multiply the area by the height.

Aunty Mabel's doorstep

Aunty Mabel's new doorstep is 5 trotters wide, 4 trotters long and 2 trotters high. What is its volume?

How many monsters?

You need to work out the volume of the carriage and divide it by 6 (the volume of a monster).

Dodo the guard wants to know how many monsters will fit in a train carriage. Can you work it out for her? The volume of one monster is 6 trotters.

Double up

Dodo and Dogosaurus are packing for their holiday. The sides of Dogosaurus' trunk each measure 1 trotter. The sides of Dodo's trunk each measure 2 trotters. Dodo claims her trunk is eight times bigger than Dogosaurus' trunk. Is this true?

The monsters decide they need an extra trunk. Its sides measure 3 trotters. How much bigger than Dogosaurus' trunk is it?

Measuring liquids

A liquid does not have a fixed shape. It borrows its shape from the container it is in.

In the Metric system liquids are measured in litres. In the Imperial system they are measured in pints and gallons.

Monsters at the Standard Measures Factory are making litre measuring jugs. A litre is the volume of water that would fill a cube measuring 10cm × 10cm × 10cm. The monsters pour a litre of water from a 10cm cube into each measuring jug. Then they mark the level on the side of the jug.

More about metric

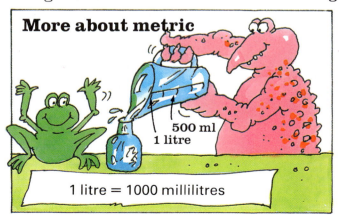

1 litre = 1000 millilitres

To measure small amounts of liquid a litre is divided into 1000 parts, called millilitres. A millilitre (ml for short) is the same as $1cm^3$ of water.

Pints and gallons

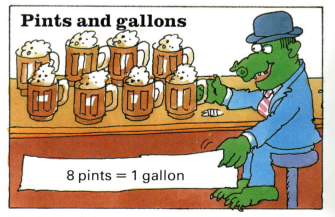

8 pints = 1 gallon

The Imperial system uses pints and gallons for measuring liquids. If you poured a pint into a litre cube it would fill it just over half way. A pint is just over half a litre.

Guessing game

Find lots of different shaped containers. Fill each container with water and try to guess how much it holds. Pour the water into a measuring jug to check your guess.

Power puzzle

Snout is motoring round Slime Island. She stops to buy 5 gallons of power juice for her monstermobile. How many pints is that?

When she was in France Snout bought power juice in litres. Can you convert 5 gallons into litres? (A pint is about half a litre.)

Bigtum's baking problem

Monsters measure liquids in units called squirts.

Bigtum needs 8 squirts of bubble juice for his new recipe. He has three measuring jugs. One will measure 9 squirts, one 3 squirts and the other 2 squirts. How can he use the three jugs to measure out 8 squirts of bubble juice?

Slopes and corners

Knowing the steepness of a slope is useful to all sorts of people. Drivers need to know when to use their brakes and hikers like to know how easy a slope is to climb.

The higher the percentage, the steeper the slope.

Dodo and Dogosaurus are walking up High Hump. When they have walked 4 trotters, they are 1 trotter higher than the bottom. You can describe this slope as 1 in 4.

Road signs often show the steepness of a hill as a percentage (a fraction of a 100). 1 in 4 is the same as 25 in 100. So as a percentage it is written like this, 25%.

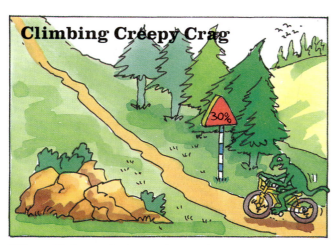

Climbing Creepy Crag

Slimy Sid wants to cycle up Creepy Crag. The steepest slope he can climb on his bike is 25%. The slope of Creepy Crag is 30%. Will Slimy Sid make it?

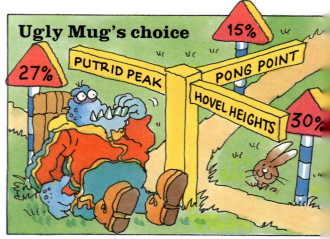

Ugly Mug's choice

Ugly Mug has the choice of climbing three mountains. He wants to climb the one with the gentlest slope – which of these three should he choose?

Angles

The angle of a corner is the amount you have to turn to go round it. Angles are measured in units called degrees, written °.

If you turn through a whole circle as Toadie has done, you turn through 360°.

If you turn a square corner, the angle is 90°. This is called a right angle.

The angle of this corner is 32°.

The angle of this corner is 100°.

The angle of this corner is 210°.

Measuring angles

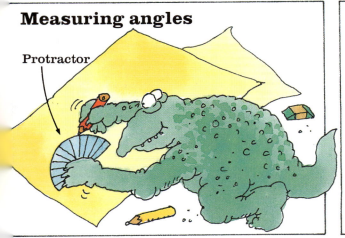

To measure or draw angles on paper you use an instrument called a protractor. A protractor is a plastic semi-circle with angles marked on it in degrees.

Guess the angle

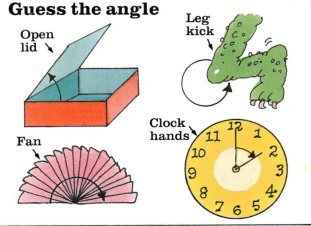

Can you tell which of these angles are bigger than a right angle (90°) and which are smaller?

Measures chart

The monsters have made a look-up chart of common Metric and Imperial measures. The short ways of writing the measures are shown in brackets.

In the Metric system measurements are always divided into 10s, 100s or 1000s. There are no particular rules for dividing measurements in the Imperial system.

Metric measures

Length
Metre (m)
Centimetre (cm)
Millimetre (mm)
Kilometre (km)

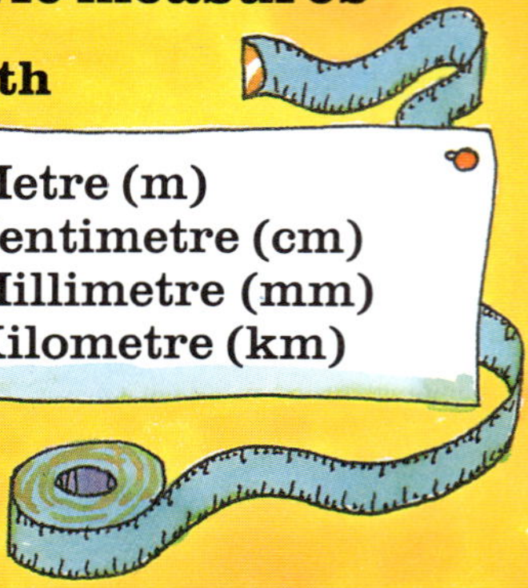

1 metre = 100 cm
1 cm = 10 mm
1 km = 1000 metres

Weight
Gram (g)
Kilogram (kg)

1 kg = 1000 grams

Area
Square metre (m^2)
Square centimetre (cm^2)
Hectare

1 m^2 = 10,000 cm^2
1 hectare = 10,000 m^2

Imperial measures

Length 
Yard (yd)
Foot (ft)
Inch (in)
Mile

1 yard = 3 ft
1 ft = 12 in
1 mile = 1760 yards

Weight
Pound (lb)
Ounce (oz)
Stone (st)

1 pound = 16 oz
1 st = 14 pounds

Stones are used in Britain for measuring a person's weight.

Area
Square yard (yd^2)
Square foot (ft^2)
Square inch (in^2)
Acre

1 yd^2 = 9 ft^2
1 ft^2 = 144 in^2
1 acre = 4840 yd^2

Travelling abroad

Here are some equivalent Metric and Imperial measures. You may find them useful if you travel abroad and have to change from one measuring system to another.

1 metre = 1.09 yards
1 km = 0.6 miles

Volume

Cubic metre (m³)
Cubic centimetre (cm³)

One million
1 m³ = 1,000,000 cm³

Liquids

Litre (l)
Millilitre (ml)

1 litre = 1000 ml

Remember a metre is just over a yard and a kilometre is just over half a mile.

Volume

Cubic inch (in³)
Cubic foot (ft³)

1 ft³ = 1728 in³

Liquids

Pint (pt)
Fluid ounce (fl oz)
Gallon (gal)

American pints and gallons are slightly smaller than British ones.

1 pint = 20 fl oz
1 gal = 8 pints

1 kg = 2.2 pounds

A kilogram is just over 2 pounds.

1 litre = 1.7 pints

1 litre is just a bit less than 2 pints.

Puzzle answers

Page 34
Ugly Mug is heavier. Bigtum's bottle holds more liquid. Hattie is taller. Dodo is hotter.

Page 37
Toga's measuring puzzle
You could use kilometres or miles to measure the distance from England to America.

The distance to the Moon is also measured in miles or kilometres.

The depth of snow on the ground is usually measured in centimetres or inches.

Dress material is measured in yards or metres.

You could use centimetres or inches to measure the size of a shirt collar.

Page 38
The monsterosa flower is 900mm high.

Don't believe your eyes!
1. These are the measurements of the lines starting with the longest.

E = 102mm
F = 89mm
D = 51mm
B = 48mm
G = 38mm
A = 25mm
C = 19mm

2. These are the lines in order of size, starting with the longest: E, C, D, B, A, F.
3. The matches are all the same size. The top match appears to be the longest because the black lines are closer at the top.

Page 39
Hattie's jellybean burger
Hattie's jellybean burger is 12 trotters high.

Page 40
Trundle puzzle
Snout's trundle wheel rotated 18 times.

Matching puzzle
A building site worker might use a trundle wheel to measure his site.
A lorry driver uses an odometer.
A dressmaker uses a tape-measure.
A decorator uses a ruler.

Page 41
How far is it?
1. It is 91 trotters from Trumpington to Hump Norton.
2. It is 155 trotters from Nottyville to Slimepool.
3. Trumpington is nearer to Trottersfield. Trumpington is 114 trotters from Trottersfield. Bogchester is 128 trotters from Trottersfield.

Mountain quiz
1. Here are the peaks in order of height: Pong Point, Fungus Tip, Putrid Peak, Hovel Heights.
2. The difference in height between Pong Point and Hovel Heights is 1,563 trotters (2,046 − 483 = 1,563).
3. If you put Putrid Peak on top of Fungus Tip, you would have a mountain as high as Pong Point (1,304 + 742 = 2,046).

Page 42
The cheese is heavier than the wool. This is because cheese is a heavier substance.

Page 43
Planet hopping
Snout would weigh:
133 blobs on Jupiter
 50 blobs on Earth
 45 blobs on Venus
 19 blobs on Mars
  8 blobs on the Moon
She weighs most on Jupiter because it is the biggest planet and least on the Moon because it is the smallest.

Page 44
Slimy Sid's trick
From left to right, the order of the labels should be flour, baking powder, sugar, salt.

Page 46
Toadie weighs 750 blobs.
Toothpeg's puzzle
Six blobs will make the scales balance.

Page 49
Ill?
The temperature of the lemon ooze is 111°C or 295.8°F.
Monster weather
1. Hump Norton will have the highest temperature.
2. Bogchester will be the coldest town.
3. Slimepool looks best for sunbathing.
4. Trumpington Lake will be best for ice skating.
5. Plodsedge will be 6°C warmer than Puddlepoint.

Page 50
Little and large
You could use cm² or in² to measure the area of a book.

The area of a snooker table would be measured in ft² or m².

A field would be measured in acres or hectares.

Page 51
Rectangle puzzle
The area of the rectangle is 20 cm².

Try these
The areas of the rectangles are:

28 m² (7 × 4 = 28)
10 m² (2 × 5 = 10)
9 m² (3 × 3 = 9)

Wiggly shapes
The area of Slime Island is about 33 square trotters. There are 25 whole squares and the pieces round the edge make about 8 squares (25 + 8 = 33).

Page 52
Monster modern art
One tin of paint will not be enough. The total area of the portrait is 49 square trotters. This is how you work it out:

Ears	$\frac{1 \times 2}{2}$	= 1
Head	3 × 5	= 15
Body	$\frac{6 \times 10}{2}$	= 30
Tail	$\frac{1 \times 3}{}$	= 3
Total		49

Grumble's new house
These are the areas occupied by Grumble's furniture:

Table	$\frac{25 \times 4}{2}$ = 50 square trotters
Sofa	9 × 5 = 45 square trotters
Rug	9 × 4 = 36 square trotters

Page 54
Measuring volume
There are 12 bales of hay each measuring 1 cubic metre, so Turniptoes is right.

Page 55
Aunty Mabel's doorstep
The volume of the doorstep is 40 cubic trotters (4 × 5 × 2 = 40).

How many monsters?
A carriage can hold 11 monsters. This is how to work it out:

Volume of carriage = 2 × 11 × 3 = 66 cubic trotters

Volume of monster = 6 cubic trotters

66 ÷ 6 = 11

Double up
It is true. Dodo's trunk is eight times bigger than Dogosaurus'.

Volume of Dogosaurus' trunk = 1 × 1 × 1 = 1 cubic trotter

Volume of Dodo's trunk = 2 × 2 × 2 = 8 cubic trotters

The volume of the third trunk is 3 × 3 × 3 = 27 cubic trotters, so it is 27 times bigger than Dogosaurus' trunk.

Page 57
Power puzzle
Five gallons are equal to 40 pints. There are 8 pints in a gallon and 5 × 8 = 40.

Five gallons are about 20 litres. To work it out you convert the gallons to pints (5 × 8 = 40). Then you need to divide by 2 because a pint is about half a litre (40 ÷ 2 = 20).

Bigtum's baking problem
To measure 8 squirts Bigtum needs to fill the 9-squirt measuring jug and pour 3 squirts from it into the 3-squirt jug. This leaves 6 squirts in the big jug. If he now adds 2 squirts from the 2-squirt jug, he will have 8 squirts of bubble juice.

Page 58
Climbing creepy crag
Slimy Sid will not make it to the top on his bike because a 30% slope is steeper than a 25% slope.

Ugly Mug's choice
Ugly Mug should climb Pong Point. Its slope of 15% is the gentlest.

Page 59
Guess the angle
The angles of the open lid and clock hands are smaller than 90°. The angles of the fan and leg kick are larger than 90°.

Index

acre, 50
angle, 59
  right, 59
area, 50-51, 52-53, 54
Aunty Mabel's doorstep, 55
Aunty Mabel's knitting, 16
balance scale, 46-47
Bigtum's baking problem, 57
Bigtum's monster cake, 6
Bigtum's shopping expedition, 3
Brain teaser, 12
calculator, 16, 18-19, 21, 22-23, 24
Celsius, 48
centigrade, 48-49
centimetre, 37, 38, 47, 50-51, 54, 60-61
circle, 53, 59
circumference, 53
Climbing Creepy Crag, 58
computer program, 6, 27, 28-29
cubes, 54, 56
cubic
  centimetre, 54, 56, 61
  foot, 61
  inch, 61
  metre, 61
decimal
  fractions, 16-17
  point, 16-17, 23
  recurring, 23, 25
degree
  of angle, 59
  of temperature, 48-49
Don't believe your eyes! 38
Double up, 55
Eratosthenes seive, 21
factors, 20
Fahrenheit, 48-49
Feet and thumbs, 36
foot, 36-37, 54, 60
fraction, 13, 24-25, 40, 58
gallon, 34, 56-57, 61
Games and guesses, 19
Gong's experiment, 44
gram, 45, 60

gravity, 43
Grumble's bubble gum, 17
Grumble's new house, 53
Guess and measure, 38
Guess the angle, 59
Guessing game, 57
Headcase and the chocobars, 11
Headcase's holiday, 15
hectares, 50, 60
Hopping backwards, 11
How far is it? 41
How heavy is Ugly Mug? 7
How many monsters? 55
Ill? 49
Imperial system, 33, 36-37, 38-39, 44-45, 56, 60-61
inch, 36-37, 38, 47, 50, 54, 60
kilogram, 45, 60, 61
kilometre, 37, 60, 61
Leap frog, 5
litre, 56-57, 60, 61
Little and large, 50
Matching puzzle, 40
metre, 37, 39, 40, 50-51, 60
Metric system, 33, 37, 38-39, 44-45, 56, 60-61
mile, 36, 37, 60
millilitre, 56, 61
millimetre, 37, 38, 60
Monster weather, 49
Monstermobile bus, 20
Monsermobile route numbers, 20
Monsterous problems, 13
Monsters' magic tables spiral, 7
Mountain quiz, 41
multiples, 6, 9, 20-21
number
  line, 4-5, 6, 11, 14
  square, 9
One more cake, 13
ounce, 44-45, 60
  fluid, 61
Party puzzle, 7
percentage, 24-25, 58
pint, 34, 56-57, 61

Planet hopping, 43
pound, 44-45, 60, 61
Power puzzle, 56
primes, 20-21
protractor, 59
radius, 53
rectangle, 50-51, 52
  puzzle, 51
remainders, 12-13, 15, 16, 18, 20
sets, 2, 5, 10
sharing, 10, 12, 13
Slimy Sid's stink bomb, 24
Snout's number trick, 19
scales, 46-47
  balance, 46, 47
  spring, 46
Stepping stones, 4
stone, 45, 60
square
  centimetre, 50-51, 60
  foot, 50-51, 60
  inch, 50-51, 60
  metre, 50-51, 60
  yard, 50-51, 60
tables, multiplication, 6-7, 8-9, 14-15, 22, 26-27, 28-29
temperature, 35, 48-49
tens, mulitiplying by, 9, 14-15, 22, 29
Tens puzzle, 9
thermometer, 48
times sign, 2
Toga's measuring puzzle, 37
triangle, 52
True or false? 20
Trundle
  puzzle, 40
  wheel, 40
Ugly Mug's choice, 58
Ugly Mug's matching game, 17
Using multiplication, 3
volume, 35, 54-55, 61
Which is bigger? 25
Wiggly shapes, 51
yard, 36-37, 40, 50-51, 60-61

First published in 1986 by Usborne Publishing Ltd, 83-85 Saffron Hill, London EC1N 8RT, England.

© 1981, 1986 Usborne Publishing Ltd.

The name Usborne and the device are Trade Marks of Usborne Publishing Ltd.

All rights reserved. No part of this publication may be reproduced, stored in a retrieval system or transmitted in any form or by any means, electronic, mechanical, photocopying, recording or otherwise, without the prior permission of the publisher.

Printed in Belgium.